The Absence of Light

Poems By
Lesley Day

Copyright © 2023 by Lesley Day

Published by Ink Soul Publishing

www.inksoulpublishing.com

inksoulpublishing@gmail.com

All Rights Reserved

Cover Design: Lesley Day

Back Cover Author Photo: Leah Manis

ISBN: 978-1-958351-02-4

This book is dedicated to my husband Chris

For without you, and the loss of you in my life, these pages would have never been written.

You will always be my favorite.

Christopher Aaron Deason

November 3, 1986 – May 11, 2014

Creative Depths

The most unique creativeness emerges from suffering.

Words of elation reach a limit,

but words that convey the raw emotion of pain

have endless depths.

Table of Contents

Dedication..1

Memory Photograph...3

Prelude Poem

Creative Depths...5

Poems

Absence of Light..13

Bareness...14

Broken Bones of My Home......................................15

The Edge of Light..19

Truth and Doubt..20

Box of Turmoil..21

Dreams..22

Rainy Tears...23

Severed Souls...24

Bound...25

Struggle in a Breath...26

Black Abyss..27

Gun Metal Box..28

Gray to Gold..29

Sinking Heart...30

Secrets in Tears..31

The Wall of Limitation......................................32

Wretched...35

I Cry Out...36

Let Me Live Once More....................................37

I Miss You...38

Lonely Soul...39

Scale...40

Blood of My Pain...42

Silent Room...44

Prayer of My Heart...45

Carried Away by a Swing..................................47

Tearflakes..49

Broken Shards..50

Foggy Streets...51

Bleak Picture...53

This Life Does Not Belong to You.....................55

Escape...58

Scarred Heart..59

Empty Shell..60

Beautiful Ashes..66

A Letter to My Daughter

To My Little Girl...69

Postscript

Acknowledgements...77

Acknowledgements Part Two...79

About the Author..81

Photographs..83

Reviews...85

Note from the Author...87

The Absence of Light

Poems

Absence of Light

Don't tell me there's nothing to fear of darkness.

Your darkness is not my own,

And apparently,

It does not contain the horrors

That haunt my absence of light.

Bareness

Sitting naked on thy bed

Limbs collapsed within

Rocking with wretched sobs

From the deepest depth of being

The chill does not touch thy bare skin

But reaches down and incases thy heart with claws of ice

Lying naked in thy bed

Limbs curled in on each other

Sobs come harder still

Causing a dry wretch from deep within

The chill has reached thy bare skin

As I lie shaking trying to find warmth

In covers that no longer keep you warm

And no longer hold your scent

Broken Bones of My Home

See me

in this brokenness.

Look down on me

on bended knee

surrounded by

the shattered fragments

of life.

As I raise my eyes,

praise isn't what comes

from my broken sobs.

Tear my throat open raw

with the screams

of angry pleas.

How the hell

do you sit back

allowing this much damage

to become my reality?

Body splayed before you
begging this tragedy
won't be
my story of life,
and that you
wake the nightmares
haunting my dreams.

Do you hear the sobs
of my desperate soul
lying among the broken bones
of my home?

No longer hidden by walls,
piece by piece
they tore them down
to the undergrowth of studs
lying exposed and bare
to hide the remnants of you
left behind.

No wife should see
white walls painted red
by her husband's death
ended with her nearby.
A gunshot still ringing
in her ears.

Despondent joists
no longer protect
my weight from gravity
as naked eyes look on
where his body laid
at final breath.

Layer after layer
ripped from the floor
that once held
our bare feet.

Seven layers deep
stolen to remove

the remnants
of your seeping blood.

Each layer a year
your blood flowed
through your veins
and pumped your heart
to the beat of living.

Seven years
your heart beat
to the beat of my own,
and was mine to love
on this forsaken earth.

Carve out every inch of evidence,
but you'll never replace
the images
branded in my mind,
or erase the memories
of happier times.

The Edge of Light

As I stand on the edge of light

I watch as the dark cloud

Descends upon the horizon

I feel the stillness surrounding me

I see the onslaught of wind and rain

Crashing its way towards me

Standing on the edge of light

I see the storm arrive

I feel the violent arms encase me

And slowly crush my soul inside

Truth and Doubt

A battle erupts

between the heart and mind.

One knows truth,

the other is a master of doubts.

Days become uncertain.

Uncertainty of who will win the day.

Who will win the hour.

Who will win each passing second.

The war wages on.

Maybe one day

the truth of the heart

will outweigh

the clever doubts of the mind.

Box of Turmoil

Tangled mess of emotions

Contained in a tiny box of turmoil

Panic comes crashing in

From a claustrophobic state

Suffocating from the weight of life

Heavier and heavier the weight bears down

It's becoming harder to breathe

In and out

In and out

Air is becoming stale

Walls quickly come closing in

Take one more shallow breath

For there's little air left to breathe

Dreams

I feel the pain of losing you

even in my dreams.

I meet you there at night

when I finally drift to sleep.

It is the only place

I hear your voice

and see your face in motion.

In every dream

you make a choice

to leave me all alone.

And so I suffer

through my dreams,

just as I suffer

when my eyes awake.

Rainy Tears

When your eyes just won't stop flowing,

sit outside and let the rain wash over you.

The sky will remind you

you're not the only one who spends days crying.

Severed Souls

Build thee a bridge

Across the gap of severed souls

That I may walk along the stones

And meet thy love once more

To stare into his clear blue eyes

And see his shining smile

To wrap thy arms around his neck

And press thy lips to his

To feel the warmth of his skin

Radiating beneath thy palms

To hear his voice say thy name

And know that he loves thee so

Build thee a bridge

Across the gap of severed souls

Bound

Lying broken in the darkness

Watchful eyes see faces

Covered with displays of smiles

This face wishes to mimic

The emotion which it sees

But the frozen planes stay rigid with emptiness

Lying in the coldness

Reaching for the light

Cutting through the sheets of despair

Straining to touch the brightness

But unable to break free from the roots

That bind thee in the thorns of this life

Struggle in a Breath

Your absence is a heavy weight

that sits upon my chest

and makes it hard to breathe.

I struggle to drag in the oxygen

to fill my lungs.

How easier it was to breathe

when I had your essence

to fill my surrounding air.

Black Abyss

The essence of time and space

has been eluded in my mind.

I'm floating in the black abyss

of crashing waves.

The water burns like flames,

as it scrapes against my lungs.

I try to open my eyes

to see what horror surrounds me,

but the salt stings my eyes,

and forces them shut into oblivion.

I feel momentary stillness in the water,

as it lightly brushes against my skin.

The stillness never lasts long,

before the storm rolls in,

bringing with it

the violent crash of waves.

I thrash back and forth

in the black abyss,

as the waves tear me apart

from the inside out.

Gun Metal Box

Sitting on the damp earth,

covered with stones of death.

Stones etched with names and dates,

of lives once lived now lost.

Staring at the mound of dirt

that now covers your silent grave.

I remember the day we came here,

to say our final goodbye.

I remember the gun metal color

of the box that held you so carefully.

I remember the tears that stung my eyes,

and stained the shiny steel.

I remember you dropping lower,

until I could no longer see.

No longer see the gun metal box

that held you so carefully.

Gray to Gold

Bare trees stretch across the land

The leaves have all fallen

And lie resting on the ground

Cold wind bites against thy soul

As the tears fall to the ground

And moisten the brittle leaves

A gray steel sky swims above thy head

The dullness matches thy inside

Give me the winter sun

And turn this gray to gold

Shine upon thy face

And dry these salty tears

Sinking Heart

This broken heart is slowly sinking,

From the weight of love and longing.

Trying to force their way out,

And seep through the cracks

That have formed over time.

Wrapped in chains and locks,

It's heavier every day.

You have the keys in your possession,

If it were only possible for you to put them to use.

You could unlock this sinking heart,

So that all the love and longing

Would pour out onto you.

Some things can never be though,

And so this locked up heart keeps sinking.

Secrets in Tears

Some days

the best thing you can do for yourself,

is to not get out of bed.

To bury yourself beneath blankets,

and let your pillow listen

to all the secrets within your tears.

The Wall of Limitation

I thought I had reached the wall

of my limitations.

I feel my face and body

pressed flush against the surface.

There's no room left

for any more damage

to come between us.

In a way,

it's almost comforting

to be pressed against that wall.

This is as bad

as it could possibly get.

I feel a light sprinkle of raindrops

start to fall from the sky.

My eyes watch

as the drops of despair

slowly hit my hand.

One,

two,

three.

Then all at once

a torrential downpour

comes crashing down.

I no longer count the drops.

My hand is now drenched.

The wall can't take the pressure

from the onslaught of rain.

With my ear flat against the surface,

I hear it began to creak.

Suddenly,

it recedes

further into the darkness.

I see the rain falling

in the gap

which now stands between us.

Confused,

my eyes stare ahead,

as the rain slowly disappears.

Behind me

the rain becomes louder,

as it comes together,

forming a towering mass at my back.

I feel the force crash into me,

stealing the breath from my lungs.

The gap quickly closes in front of me.

I'm once again

slammed up against the wall,

even further away than before.

Wretched

There's crying,

And there's screaming.

And then

There's the heartbroken wailing

That comes from some wretched place

Deep inside,

I never even knew existed.

I Cry Out

Here we go again,

Another restless night without sleep.

Oh Yeshua,

Why must I be tormented

To the point of insanity?

My mind is disheveled,

I cannot handle this my Lord.

These pills make me uneasy.

On a ledge am I,

Ready to fall to my death.

Oh Lord,

Do you not hear my cries?

Do you not taste my tears?

Do you not see my pain?

I cry out to you, oh Lord.

Please Yeshua,

Save me!

Let Me Live Once More

I lie down outside

On a cold winter night

I'm unable to think

Unable to see

Blind and confused

Wipe away the black clouds

That haunt my dark world

Cleanse this heart of mine

And let me live once more

I Miss You

I miss you every day,

but some days the absence of you in my day

is all consuming.

Lonely Soul

Dark clouds consume the sky

With cracks of brightness fighting through

The rays of sun shine through the clouds

And reach their arms towards the earth

To touch the lonely soul

The lonely soul that finds itself

Hiding beneath crooked limbs

Trimmed in evergreen

Close to the ragged edge

That looks down upon

Still waters cool and deep

Waters that sing a promise

To take away the pain

Scale

Some days

I just want

To give up.

It's all too much.

It's everything,

And everything

Is really

Nothing at all.

I feel as though

I'm not enough,

And too much

All at once.

I wonder

If the goodness I have,

Is enough to outweigh

The darkness and scars

That live inside.

There's a

Teetering scale,

And I fear the latter

Will win the day.

Blood of My Pain

My week comes to an end

A crash and burn

The flames of my life rising high in the air

Everything has gone to hell

These days I live seem unreal

I can't escape

Everywhere I turn

The despair is there

Everything has been ruined again and again

No longer can I control myself

Tears flow down from my eyes

My mind and body are uneasy

As they always are

My life is tearing at the seams

My face ugly now

From smeared black make-up

Dripping from my swollen eyes

I am a weak link unable to breathe

Trying so hard to be strong

So as not to be seen as the insane person I am

I have tried so hard to see your face

I can't find it

For I am lost

How could I

The broken disheveled girl that I am

Ever be loved by you

My dreams for my life are too far fetched

Silent Room

Sitting in the middle of a silent room,

With cold blank walls and blinding lights.

Depression grabs a hold of me,

And I lose all hope.

The walls come crashing down,

Yet there is no sound.

My efforts to hold them up fail,

As I sit shaking in the middle

Of that still so silent room.

Prayer of My Heart

Hold me together

Oh God.

Knit my heart and soul

Back together,

So that I may feel

Whole again.

Wrap your arms

Around my being,

And hold me tight,

So I don't fall to pieces.

Place your hands

Over my eyes,

So that I might only see

What pleases you.

Hear my cry

In the crowds

Of screaming voices.

The quiet ache

Of a shattered heart.

Rain down your grace

On me,

So that one day

I'll be able to use

Your healing love

To rain down on others.

Tragedy has left me

Feeling dry.

Fill me to the point

Of overflowing.

Oh God,

Calm the storm in my soul.

Carried Away by a Swing

Two tattered ropes

hang from an old tree,

tied to a rough slab of wood.

A makeshift swing,

made by a young girl.

There was a time

when troubled thoughts

could be carried away

by the rush of wind in her ears.

Taken away by the burning muscles,

as her legs pumped harder,

and the swing flew higher.

Comfort in the feel

of a tangled mess of brown curls

covering her face from view,

as the swing reaches the branches above,

and her bare feet

brush against the rough leaves.

The troubled thoughts

of that young girl,

are not the thoughts

that haunt her mind today.

There are some thoughts,

the rush of wind on a swing

can't even momentarily carry away.

Tearflakes

Tear drops fall

Like the winter snow

My tears are the flakes

Each different and unique

Snowflakes melt away

The same as my tears

Each one lost and forgotten

To everyone but me

Broken Shards

Broken shards of this soul

Are scattered around this life

Piece by piece they're glued in place

Until it looks like something whole

But when I stare at this soul

This is what I see

I see broken shards of this soul

Pieced together in deformity

Foggy Streets

We walk together

Down foggy streets

Drenched in sheets of rain

I hold each of your tiny hands

Tightly inside mine

Three pairs of walking feet

Splash with every step

You're looking up at me

With dripping faces and searching eyes

Eyes that seek an answer

To the reason why

Our life became consumed

With all these foggy streets

Drenched in sheets of rain

Looking at your little faces

I wish I had your answer

But all I have to offer

Are these hands of mine

They will continue to hold your tiny hands

Tightly inside mine

Until the fog fades away

And sun replaces the rain

Bleak Picture

These people come to take the space left by destruction,

and minimize the damages done.

People always fade away though.

Time slowly takes them away,

one by one,

until we're left with none.

Once the crowd subsides,

and the debris has settled,

a bleak picture lies before me.

A picture that has been cut to pieces,

but none of the pieces

fit together again quite right.

Pain, loss, tragedy, trauma, and blood.

Three sets of sad eyes,

some more confused than others.

Three broken hearts,

and love.

Broken hearts

that have to try to put the picture back together,

and understand

that the scorched missing pieces

will never come back

to make the picture complete.

This Life Does Not Belong to You

You have a want

for me to be confined

to sheets and pain.

To fall

into a dark hole,

and never come out.

To see no light

at the end

of this bleak tunnel.

To stand staring

at the shattered fragments

of life.

This life

does not belong

to you.

I will not

be confined

to sheets and pain.

I choose to live.

I choose

to find my way

out of the sheets,

and find a sense of joy.

I will climb my way out

of this dark hole,

even if I emerge

with bloody scrapes.

I'll strain my tired eyes,

until I see the speck of light

at the end

of this bleak tunnel.

I choose to slowly

pick up the shattered fragments,

and put them back

into some semblance of order.

I refuse

to stand staring,

and succumb

to a broken life.

Escape

Press hard against the weight

that lies across your chest.

Push through the burning pain

that holds your body hostage.

Squint through the foggy tears

that have momentarily blinded your eyes.

Find the forgotten path

that leads to your escape.

Scarred Heart

God can mend and heal a broken heart.

He can take a needle and thread,

and stitch it together to make it whole again.

The scars of tragedy

cannot be erased from this heart though.

They will always shine through,

and be a part of my being.

So take my scarred heart as it is,

or simply leave it be.

Empty Shell

A therapist sits across from me in a chair

whose pattern has become all too familiar

to my avoidant eyes.

His words warning

a person can only take so much,

before that person will break.

Attempting to make preparations

for the inevitability

of the breaking point

I must meet.

His wondering mind forms anxiety,

as every week he packs his toolbox

in anticipation

that this will be the session,

this will be the day,

this will be the time

that I finally meet my break.

As if his tools

are only worthy to fix

his perception

of the upmost destruction.

I don't understand the meaning behind his words.

His eyes take in the sight of my figure,

but he must be blind to what he sees.

His ears process the words that come from my mouth,

but he must be ignorant to their meaning.

I have been shattered into tiny slivers,

and continually bleed from the cuts

my own body makes in betrayal

of continuing to live,

as it struggles to move forward with time,

every moment of the day.

He registers my lack of understanding,

just as I have registered his.

I ask him what it is he is waiting for.

He tells me there will come a day,

when I will be unable

to pull myself out of bed

to face whatever that day will hold,

and not even the voices of my children

will keep me from being succumbed

by the darkness of this strange windowless room,

where I now attempt to sleep.

My body will be consumed

by the coldness of pillows and blankets,

and the mattress lying on the floor,

waiting with a gaping mouth

hungry to swallow me whole.

The void of unending darkness

will be too much

for what is left of me to bear,

and I will give up

on this functional level of life

that I have been living.

His words attempt the warmth of a hope
he pushes across the room to reach me,
with words that this will be a temporary stage,
but I must understand
this is a stage that will come.

Catching the false warmth of hope,
and grasping it between my fingers,
I crush it within my palms,
and watch as the fragmented pieces
fall to the empty space between us.
For this hope
of his misconstrued version
of temporary breaking,
is not a hope
that I need.

Giving up
the functionality of living
is not a luxury
I possess.

For mine is not the only heart that grieves,

but it is the only heart big enough,

to hold the grief of the rest.

A grieving mother has no option,

but to act the part of living,

until she becomes a master of technique,

waiting for the lines of act and reality,

to blur back into one.

Is this misconstructed idea of brokenness

the definition believed

by those who look at me,

and tell me that I am strong?

What will it take to convince them

my body has become a fragile empty shell,

with only specks of salt

to show the remnants of evidence

of the beauty of an ocean

that once rushed through

its open soul

filling it to its brim?

Put your ear to this seashell chest,

and I promise you will only hear

the faint empty echo

of the crashing waves

that once lived inside.

But broken bodies still move,

shattered hearts still beat,

damaged minds still think,

and empty seashells

still make a sound.

Beautiful Ashes

Take this simple life

Scorched by burning fires.

Take this simple body

Reduced to bone and ash.

Take this life and body,

Destroyed by tragedy.

Take them in your hands,

And make beautiful these ashes.

A Letter to My Daughter

To My Little Girl

Adelaide James

As your mom,

the thing I struggle with more than anything else,

is not being able to take away your pain.

If it were possible,

I would take every shred of your pain,

and stitch it into my heart,

so that you may never know the force

of its wicked blows.

Unfortunately,

I'm only able to share your pain,

and cannot blot it out.

Since there's not an easy escape for your tiny little heart,

I want you to remember these few simple,

yet sometimes difficult things.

Remember that it is okay to feel broken.

It is okay to be sad.

To feel angry at anything and everything.

It's okay to feel jealous

when your friends and cousins talk about their daddy.

It's okay to be angry that yours is no longer here.

It is okay to ask for help.

Please, always ask for help.

It is okay to not be okay,

but it is also okay to be happy.

One day you may feel like blaming someone.

It might be your dad,

for leaving you much too soon.

Or maybe you'll blame God,

for taking him away.

That someone you may blame,

at one time or another may even be me.

Sweetie, that's okay too,

but eventually you must always choose to forgive,

no matter how hard it may be.

Don't ever let your anger make a home inside.

You're entitled to visit all these dark places,

and feel the emotions they bring,

but just remember

to never stay there too long.

There were those that said I was weak,

and wrong to let you see my pain.

That somehow,

by letting you see my tears and hear my screams,

I would hurt your fragile heart.

They may be right,

but I personally believe they're wrong.

You were only three

when your world was ripped apart,

but you were intelligent and perceptive

way beyond your years,

and that fragile heart was already broken

into a hundred little pieces.

I didn't want to hide what I was,

from you,

who needed me most.

I wanted you to see what was real,

and not some fabricated front.

I wanted you to see that your mommy

could not always be strong.

I wanted you to know that in our house,

crying about Daddy was always allowed.

And if you felt like screaming

about how it's just not fair,

that's something you just have to do.

But baby, this doesn't make us weak.

You saw me broken,

but you saw me fight to find the light.

You saw the smiles and laughter

that shone in the darkness

that surrounded our lives.

You see,

I believe that knowing when to be weak,

is part of being strong.

And admitting you need help,

is part of being wise.

Being strong isn't about always being straight faced,

or bright smiles.

Being strong is facing your pain,

and not burying it deep inside.

You can smile through the tears,

but be sure to let them fall.

And you can giggle through the anger,

but take the time to also scream it to the sky.

Don't keep any of that bottled up inside.

I know you have many questions.

The how's and why's and what's.

I know you hate to hear

that you're just too young to understand,

but I promise to answer what I can,

and some day when you're older,

I'll give you every answer I have.

When that day does come,

it will bring a whole lot of new pain,

and I want you to know I'm sorry

that you'll feel the things you will.

Your road will not be easy,

but I will be right beside you

every step of the way.

You have many more sticks and stones

than others you may know.

You will trip,

and you will fall,

and you'll bleed a lot along the way,

but you little girl will rise,

wash yourself off

and continue on your way.

You will not only live,

but you will conquer the life that you have.

I have seen your strength,

and the heavy weight

that sits upon those tiny shoulders,

and you little girl,

have a mighty warrior inside.

January 1, 2017

Acknowledgements

Thank you to my husband Chris for giving me a great love that will last me a lifetime. With such great love, there is great pain in the loss. The grief of losing you broke me in ways I didn't know were possible, but I think you would be proud of how I not only survived, but how I've thrived. Time may have only given us 6 years, 11 months, and 5 days together on this earth, but our love will never fit within the confines of time.

Thank you to my daughters Adelaide and Athena. Although you were only babies when our world was ripped apart, you held me up, and took care of me in more ways than you could ever know. From tiny toddler hugs and kisses to stop my tears, to being the most thoughtful and caring daughters through all these years. You've seen me at my very darkest, but I hope in seeing that darkness, you learned that no matter how shattered a soul can become, those pieces can be put back together, and one day the light of happiness will shine through again. You both healed me more than I thought was possible, and you have made this life a beautiful one, even in the midst of the tragedy that touched our lives.

Thank you to my besties Tammy and Sarah for our weekly coffee dates you gave me when I needed you most, and continuing them all of these years. They truly are the most beneficial therapy I've ever received. I would not be where I am today without your unconditional friendship, love, and support. You made it possible for me to follow my biggest dreams.

A special thank you to my mom for her never ending love and support, and for always being there to listen and calm my frustrations and tears. You will forever be my first call on my hardest days. Thank you for raising me to believe in myself and my talents. For never diminishing my love of writing, or discouraging my dream of publishing one day. More than anyone, you made my success a possibility, by never thinking it was too big of a dream.

Thank you to all the family and friends that were there to hold me up and support me through the darkest days of my life. Thank you for helping my girls and I find healing in this beautiful broken life.

Thank you to my Title Composer Lindsey Asher, for always listening to my poems, and coming up with the perfect title for the pieces that my intermittent creative mind can't find a title for.

Thank you to all my readers and listeners! Thank you for every purchase, every review, every recommendation given, every social media share, comment and like, and for every performance and event attended! Your overwhelming support has made my work a success, and this new collection a reality. Thank you for your patience in waiting for it to finally be released, through all the struggles and delays.

Lastly, thank you to my journals that held the heaviness of my broken soul, and my pens that bled my pain upon their pages. Thank you for holding the messiness of my hand scrawled ink, which one day becomes books upon shelves.

Acknowledgements

Part Two

The poem *Bareness* was previously published in Eber & Wein Publishing's anthology *Beyond the Sea – Mystique.*

About the Author

Photo Credit: Jenn Deason   Edited By: Lesley Day

Lesley Day is the author of the poetry collections *Authenticity*, *The Absence of Light*, and *IMPACT – A Woman's Story from Surviving to Living* from *Ink Soul Publishing*, as well as the *Love Me Don't Leave Me* poetry collection that was written in collaboration with the *Love Me Don't Leave Me* painting series by artist Leisa Collins. Day has also had her poetry published in several anthologies, and has had multiple articles published in online magazines.

Although poetry is her main passion, Day is also a writer of children's literature, personal essays, articles, fiction, non-fiction, and the occasional blogging. Her topics include mental illness, grief, trauma, insomnia, adventure, dreams, nature, and mommyhood. More than anything though, her writing encompasses the chaos of her mind, and the passions of her soul.

In 2014, at the age of twenty-five, Lesley tragically lost her husband, and became a widow and single mommy to her two young daughters. Through the years she's worked tirelessly to heal her soul, and to gather all their broken pieces in her hands, to create an unexpected, yet still beautiful life. Although their lives will always be stained by grief, trauma, pain, and hardships that never seem to stop coming, Day has managed to give herself and her daughters a life that is also full of happiness, laughter, adventures, and chasing dreams.

When she's not camping on the river, hiking trails, traveling around the world, swimming in oceans, climbing mountains, or taking cross country road trips, Day spends most of her days juggling the complete chaos that comes with writing, publishing, working multiple jobs, and most of all, raising two sassy little girls and one silly little pupkid.

Day travels all around performing her poetry, but her home is in a small town in Missouri, where she lives with her little misfit family.

Praise for the
Authenticity Collection
By Lesley Day

"It will steal your breath, and stab your heart at the same time... This collection of poems is filled with raw, honest, heart-wrenching pieces that will break down all your walls and settle in a part of your heart. They are unforgettable. The anguish, the pain, the trauma... You can feel it all as you read." – Sarah D.

"A profoundly brave endeavor by the author, Authenticity explores grief, insomnia, mental illness, gender roles, beauty, and - above all - the life of a reader. While a good chunk of the poems feel more like a poetry-prose hybrid, it does not tire the reader with overly-flower language, and meandering lines of description. Her collection is both meditative and quarrelsome. The author transposes a broad range of emotions over a spectrum of life experiences with effectively frank verbiage, and, at times, conversational tone. Day's writing is defiant, insightful, bullish, imaginative, full of heartache, and of course - authentic. A powerful read, and a worthy piece of literature. The world is better with this book in it." – Scott Wisdom, Independent Director & Filmmaker

"Lesley Day's book is searing in its honesty in a way that makes your heart feel every word of Day's poetry." – Dunaway Books

"This is a powerful collection of lived experiences told in vivid, exquisite phrasing that only the poetic form can deliver, and yet, this writing is not out of the reach of the average reader. There is nothing pretentious about these poems, and each one cradles the pain and beauty of a hurting and healing heart. That truly requires exceptional skill to accomplish, and Ms. Day has just that kind of talent. I read this, in Kindle version, cover to cover as soon as I got it, each page evoking powerful emotion and empathy for the challenges the author has transformed into this creative work. Her descriptions often make a breath-taking turn of the sort that will leave other poets just a little bit envious."
- Deah Curry, Author of *Creating Sanity in Troubling Times*

"The author's emotions were quite literally dripping off of the pages, and I could so easily empathize with how they were feeling throughout." – Jake L.

"I could have escaped for hours, days with this little book of poetry and if I had one criticism it would be that I was left wanting more. Googling her name as if I'd find more passages to satiate that part of myself that holds my own madness. My own survival. My own understanding. Because I found all of those things within the pages.

This is the type of read that can only come from a place of truth, and not the modern day cliches' where the word "truth" gets thrown around in meaningless generalizations; but the type of truth that we can't define with our own words, a place where fact and fiction toe a fine line, a place where genius and the point of insanity meet in this combustion of REAL TRUTH. Real truth that can only be experienced and never duplicated... but somehow, SOMEHOW Lesley managed to convey it in the way that only an artist can. Passages from her lines sticking with me for always, ready to take their spot amongst the greats.

Make no mistake. This is a raw and gritty read- and it's easy to identify the authors growth as well as regression, the seesaw of both swinging back and forth as she conveys her experience of her own life, one filled with unspeakable tragedy, humility, grace, understanding, and the freedom of forgiveness." - Amanda

"The writings contained in this book, will touch you. There will be lines that seem like the writer just pulled them directly from your head. Lesley has a style of writing that is easy to feel and easy to identify with." – Christina G.

"Day is incredibly expressive and articulate, painting pictures with her words. She takes you on a journey with visits to poignant moments in her life. Her observations are insightful." Mary C.

"How the author can create such lyrical assimilation from absolute chaos, making the reader feel her pain and healing all at the same time is simply profound!" – B. McMillen

Note from the Author

Reviews play a big part in a book's success, especially a book by an indie author, or published by an indie press! If you like what you've read, or even if you didn't, all honest reviews are greatly appreciated! Thank you!

- Lesley Day

You can find more of my books on Amazon, and at select bookstores and libraries!

If you'd like to follow me on social media, you can find me by searching **@lesleydaypoetry**.

Visit my website **lesleydaywriting.com** for more updates and content.

Made in the USA
Monee, IL
20 November 2023